Dogs are often said to be 'man's best friend'. They were the first animal to be domesticated, that is to live with us in our homes. Over a very long time, dogs have been bred to be completely different shapes and sizes, and trained to do many different jobs.

Adult Newfoundlands can be as much as 60kg and 69cm high.

Adult French mastiffs can be as much as 60kg and 65cm high.

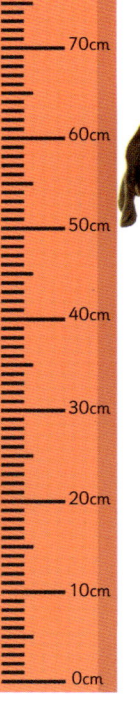
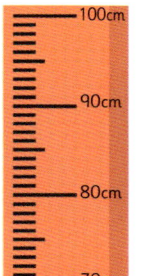

Adult toy poodles are only 3.5kg and 26cm high.

Adult pugs are only 7.5kg and 30cm high.

A dog can detect more high-pitched sounds than we can.

A dog's sense of smell is about 100,000 times stronger than ours.

Dogs are omnivores. They use their sharp teeth to eat meat, vegetables and grains.

Unlike us, dogs can only sweat from their paws.

Dogs are very agile. They can complete complex agility courses.

Dogs normally have between one and twelve pups in a litter, but one mastiff had a litter consisting of 24 pups!

mother mastiff

pups suckling milk

For the first two to three weeks, the pups are helpless because they are deaf and cannot see. They suckle milk from their mother until they are ready to start eating solid food.

mastiff pups

Mother dogs lick their pups to keep them clean.

Some pups do not look like the adult dogs when they are born. Dalmatians (/dal**mai**shenz/) are completely white when they are born. Their spots develop as they grow.

Farmers use dogs to help herd and protect their animals.

These sheepdogs are sent to gather up the sheep. The farmer uses whistles and specific commands to tell the dogs what to do.

Dogs are very loyal, and will protect their owners. This makes them excellent at guarding houses and other buildings.

When dogs bark, they can sound very frightening.

In the Arctic, dogs have been bred to help with sledges. The husky is the commonest breed of sledge dog. A husky normally has pale blue eyes, but it can have green, brown or amber eyes, and some dogs even have mismatched eyes!

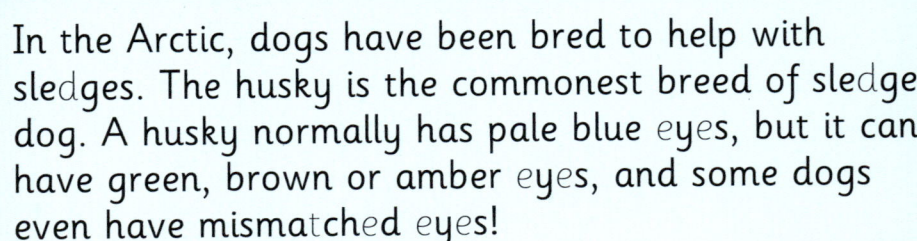

husky pup

adult husky

A husky howls instead of barking. Husky dogs have very thick coats. Originally, they lived outside all the time, even when it was snowing.

A team of dogs is used to drag a sledge. The sled driver shouts, 'mush' to make the team go quicker.

Dogs have an extremely good sense of smell. They are excellent at following a scent, which is why they were once used for hunting and why they are now used to help to search for missing persons.

Dogs can even sense someone trapped under a collapsed building.

One of the best-known breeds of rescue dog is the Saint Bernard. The first ever rescue dogs are also believed to have been Saint Bernards. These dogs first helped to rescue travellers in the Swiss Alps in around 1670.

These 'K-9 officers' chase and attack criminals, sniff out evidence, and protect and defend their handlers. Many service dogs have been given medals for bravery.

a service dog

a service dog training to catch criminals

Sniffer dogs are trained by the customs service to sniff out drugs, and by the army to sniff for bombs and landmines.

a sniffer dog sniffing for drugs

Guide dogs are trained to help those who cannot see. The dogs are selected for guide dog training when they are still young pups.

These pups are about to start their training.

After about thirty weeks' training, the dogs are ready to leave guide dog school, and live with their new owners.

a guide dog in training

Labradors are often used as guide dogs, because they are intelligent and gentle.

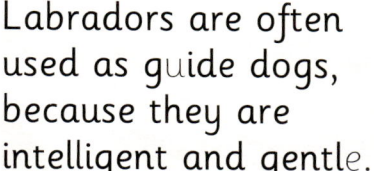

Labrador guide dog

This dog is helping its owner get around

Dogs are also trained to help those who are deaf and those who have an illness or disability.

Some dogs are used for 'pet therapy'. They are taken into hospitals and care homes by their owners to visit those who live there. The residents love to see, pet and play with the dogs. Some dogs even go into schools so that the children can read to them!

Now you can see why dogs are called 'man's best friend'.